# *Follow My Pen*

## Inspiration

Tiffani R. Addison

Copyright © 2016 Tiffani Addison

**Follow My Pen Publishing**

**FollowMyPen.com**

Vol. 1

All rights reserved. No Part of this book may be produced, stored in a retrieval system, or transmitted in any form or by any means, electronic, mechanical, photocopying, recording, or otherwise, without prior consent from the copyright holder.

**Author** Tiffani Addison

**Design by** Charon Timmons

**Illustration by** Taylor Slade

**Author Photography by** Joel Adrian Harris

**Back Cover Photography by** Marcus McCurtis

All rights reserved.

ISBN-10: **1530453887**
ISBN-13: **978-1530453887**

*"Gracious words are a honeycomb, sweet to the soul and healing to the bones."*

***Proverbs 16:24***

Dedicated to Mary and Emory—the two people who taught me about God, love, loyalty and respect—who encouraged me to follow my dreams and showed me how—who have loved me unconditionally—and who taught me that "What you are is God's gift to you, but what you become is your gift to God," and that "It's not in your hips, lips and fingertips that make you a woman."

Thank you mommy and daddy!

## *Family*

Family. Is supposed to be a unit of people whom you can remove all of your layers around. Not worry about being examined, judged or deceived. People who know where you're coming from, who know your heart and soul, so can empathize with you. Pray for you and stand by you.

The criticism, judgments and competitiveness is left to the rest of the world. With family you should be able to let your hair down, relax, not be on trial, or taken advantage of, but filled with hope, love, encouragement and positivity.

A place where you can recharge from what the world daily drains. People who want to see you succeed and excel. Where they won't always have the answers but will connect to the source that does, for you. Family is a unit specifically designed by God. Where He is the center. And when the world tries to steal your focus, God is where you all look, to regain it.

Of all people in this world each of you have not only seen but experienced the worst and best times with one another. Where you don't have to prove a thing, because past the social status, physical appearances and age differences, you know the true soul of one another.

The family should be the safe haven, a safe house during the storms and hard times. Where your weakness and your secrets disappear. Where you forget about the hardships of life and time stands still. Where records of wrong don't exist. Where you're helping hand never gets tired. Where accounts are lost. And Love never runs out.

*Inspiration*

The family encourages you to do and be your best, because when there is a sickness it affects the entire body. We are strong when we are one. Together we will stand and divided we can't.

Follow My Pen

## ***Truth + Justice***

Man has spent so much time and so many years trying to control one another.

We did not create ourselves.

We did not put ourselves into this universe.

We do not possess all of the answers.

We have spent so much time and energy trying to develop a system of hierarchy and control, division and capitalism.

That same energy has the power to heal.

We are all one body in the human race. We are born the same and when we die we are the same.

Our bodies are all flesh and blood and bones.

When we degrade, destroy and separate each other we only inflict curse and harm on ourselves.

We are not separated by skin color, language, religion and education, we are bonded by spirit.

We are so much more powerful when we connect to the higher and infinite power of our creator.

*Inspiration*

In the end, the measure of cruelty, injustice and hatred will be measured back to those who distributed it, participated in it, and those who stood by idly and watched it.

Every right will be wronged, every tear will be dried, every hurt will be forgotten, every evil will be destroyed, every truth will prevail and every justice will be served.

## ***Judgement.***

The level of self-righteousness our society embodies is nauseating. As if we all have not/will not make mistakes. Sadly, while good can be spread, social media also provides the weak-minded and insecure a stage for foolery, ignorance, competitiveness and hatred.

The facades of perfection attempted to be portrayed, along with the un-researched opinions, are laughable. Finding comfort in the misfortune of others highlights the depth of evil and emptiness this world possesses.

"Do not judge others, and you will not be judged. For you will be treated as you treat others. The standard you use in judging is the standard by which you will be judged. And why worry about a speck in your friend's eye when you have a log in your own?" Matthew 7:1-3

*Inspiration*

## *<u>I Wonder Why...</u>*

I wonder why the longer we live, it seems, the less we know...

I wonder why we complicate such simplicity...

I wonder why we spend so much time trying to figure out a problem that has already been solved...

I wonder why we search for the answers when they have already been given...

I wonder why we fight each other when that only destroys ourselves...

I wonder why we tear down the ones we love in an attempt to build ourselves...

I wonder why we give so much energy to black holes that don't give it back...

I wonder why we love those that don't love us back...

I wonder why we give to those that only take but only take from those that give...

I wonder why we strive to appear holy instead of actually achieving it...

I wonder why we focus so much on this life when this life is not even the focus...

I wonder why we care so much about the things that don't care for us...

I wonder why we try so hard to be everything except what we are...

I wonder why we hate everything that is good and turn everything that is good into something we hate...

I wonder why we push away what we need but invite what we don't...

I wonder why we say we want what's best for each other but get mad when we actually get it...

I wonder why we feel that our way is the best way...

I wonder why we love comfort and fear change...

I wonder why we have a hard time being happy for one another...

Follow My Pen

Is it because we secretly hate ourselves…

Don't you see, that your success is directly tied to the body, and if the body fails, so do you…

Hatred and envy grow from inside, sadly destroying the giver not the receiver…

Trying to shadow someone's light only dims your own, while allowing theirs to illuminate through you…

Haven't you realized by now, that the key to everything you desire is how you love yourself and one another…?

So, I wonder…

*Inspiration*

## ***Words***

"But I tell you that men will have to give account on the Day of Judgment for every careless word they have spoken. For by your words you will be acquitted, and by your words you will be condemned."

Matthew 12:36-37

## ***Fall***

Research shows that "in romantic relationships, falling in love is the concept of moving from a feeling of neutrality towards a person to one of love."

"The use of the term "fall" implies that the process is in some way uncontrollable and risky – as in the phrases "to fall ill" or "to fall into a trap" – and that it leaves the lover in a state of vulnerability."

"Factors known to contribute strongly to falling in love include proximity, similarity, reciprocity, and physical attractiveness," while at the same time, the process involves a re-activation of old childhood patterns of attachment. Deep-set psychological parallels between two people may also underpin their pairing-bonding, which can thus border on mere narcissistic identification."

The process is quick.<br>
There's a blink and then a punch.<br>
It hits you, and you're in it.<br>
Surrounded by it.<br>
Consumed in it.<br>
Driven by it.<br>
Inspired by it.<br>
Pulled by it.<br>
Pushed by it.<br>
It lifts you to your highest point.<br>
It can take you to your lowest point.<br>
It makes you courageous.<br>
The world becomes your playground.

*Inspiration*

There is NOthing you can't do.
You believe that you can conquer anything.
It is all within your reach.
You become in-tune with the earth.
You become one with mankind.
You are more patient.
You are more kind.
You are more selfless.
You are not blind.
Your senses are keener than ever.
Your strength is incomparable.
When two join as one in spiritual harmony.
You experience the fragrance from heaven on earth.

Fall. In Love.

*Follow My Pen*

"ART WASHES AWAY FROM THE SOUL THE DUST OF EVERYDAY LIFE."

-Pablo Picasso

*Inspiration*

## ***The Skin vs Within***

While you're focused on the tone of your skin, or the length and texture of your hair, are you effectively changing the world? How do these factors truly play a part? Believing that it adds validation to your being and existence… or that it takes it away, makes you as guilty as those who persecute others for being outside of their comfort zone.

How does a male that states that he despises a woman of the same skin tone as his own — or darker/lighter — have the capability of truly and fully loving anyone else? When it is evident that he does/ cannot love himself.

What about the woman who supports these stereotypical insecurities of self-hatred and send destructive behavior? What is she thinking? What does this say about her self-esteem, self-worth and self-love?

To hate your own skin is to hate yourself, your mother and father who made you, your brothers and sisters around you, your ancestors who lived so you could live, and the God who created you…

So, again I ask, how does the color of your skin determine your worth on this earth… when in the end we all will she'd these shells to reveal a spirit of either darkness or light…

You will endure hardships on this earth no matter what… you decided whether you will be the contributor to adversity or the solution.

## *Truth is...*

When I think about the persecution of Christians it saddens my heart... Not because we are innocently murdered, but because the killers are so lost that they actually believe killing Christians is going to solve their problems. *("For to me, to live is Christ and to die is gain..." Philippians 1:21)* Let's examine this for just a moment... What instance has there ever been where Christians bombed a building full of innocent people, or shot young adults on a college campus because they believe in Jesus Christ, or killed young children in Sunday school, or fellowshipped with another religious group during one of their weekly meetings and then shot and killed all of them when it was over. How many times are Christians laughed at for our beliefs and made a mockery of, yet never to retaliate with that same violence or by returning the hate? *("Blessed are you when people insult you, persecute you and falsely say all kinds of evil against you because of me..." Matthew 5:11)* I find it interesting that as a peaceful group of believers, missioned for oneness, wholeness and unity, we are targeted with the exact opposite... The moment that we proclaim we are believers in the Holy Bible and Jesus Christ, we are immediately ridiculed and hated. Despite everyone's "cry" for individuality and acceptance we receive the opposite, immediately judged and put under the radar and microscope to be dissected and picked apart. Has anyone ever asked themselves, why? Why do I hate them so much? Why do the words of the bible get under my skin and touch my soul? If something is completely untrue and irrelevant, why am I affected by it? None of us claim to have written the words in the Bible but we believe in a higher power that did. This power causes us to want to live in peace, whole and pure. We don't judge those that do not live by the words we just pray for them, live by example and hope that they too will one day arrive at this place of peace, fullness and unity. *("But I say*

*to you who hear, love your enemies, do good to those who hate you, bless those who curse you, pray for those who mistreat you. Whoever hits you on the cheek, offer him the other also; and whoever takes away your coat, do not withhold your shirt from him either..."*
*Luke 6:28)* We are driven to live differently, in a way that causes us to turn the other cheek, to pray for those who curse us, and to love one another despite our differences. THIS is how you show love, is by being it. What are persecutors do not realize or understand is that this life is not the end for us. It's a blessing and an opportunity to be light in such a dark, dishonest, selfish and evil world. Despite those who take judgment into their own hands and play the part of God, we are purposed to be love and light, not condemnation to the world, our Savior will do that. We can only continue to hope and pray, that one day, we will all see the light, and we will all be free, from hurt, pain, and darkness.

Amen.

*"Then you will know the truth, and the truth will set you free..." John 8:32*

## ***Food for thought…***

When you're in competition with yourself you'll never lose…

*Inspiration*

## <u>*Who Are You...*</u>

Every tear watered the heart of the earth.

Every smile reflected the rays of the sun.

Every laugh gave the birds a song to echo.

Every prayer released God's grace into man.

Every heartbreak quaked the earth and woke the thunder.

Every moment of righteousness blessed another generation.

Every moment of silent strength defeated a layer of darkness.

Every intercession unlocked a higher realm of heaven.

Every sacrifice planted another rose in the garden of eternity.

We are the beat in God's heart. He divinely set us apart. He saved the best for last. Focus on your future and learn from your past. Put back on your crown, no more holding your head down. You are a daughter of The Creator. There is no one greater. God loves you. There is no other above you. You are one of a kind. He looks at you and says, "She's Mine!" You are woman! ♥

## ***Win to Lose...***

Why do we lose time to gain money…

Why do we gain money, just to lose it…

Why do we gain others and lose ourselves…

Why do we gain things and lose people…

Why do we feel alone when it's crowded…

Why do we want more than we give…

Why do we give less than we take…

Why do we hide truth but encourage lies…

Why do we believe in greatness while displaying mediocrity…

Why do we say work hard just to be lazy…

Why do we accept ignorance over wisdom…

Why do we dismiss good and invite evil…

Why do we ask for all just to answer some…

Why do we claim to be kings while living like peasants…

Why do we hunger for the future while pushing away the present…

Why do we drain the weak and add to the strong…

*Inspiration*

Why are our actions for short while wanting to live long…

Why do we hate correction but accept defeat…

Why do we neglect to train but fear being weak…

Why do we despise being alone but abandon companionship…

Why do we ask for a friend but live in independence…

Why must we go against the grain…

Are we all insane…

Why do we accept defeat…

Why won't we do what's right…

Why do we quiet the meek…

Why are we afraid to be nice…

Why do we journey to death…

Why don't we choose life…

Why do we ignore what's next…

Why don't we understand that it is our power to choose…

Why do we live… to die… to win… to lose…

Follow My Pen

## ***Now That I Have Your Attention…***

We live in a world where right is believed to be wrong and wrong is believed to be right. Shameful is proud and there's no holiness in sight. Opinions mean more than facts. Truth is mistaken for lies. Laughter is transformed into cries. Ugly is called beautiful and meekness cannot be found. Darkness is ruling and lights are dim. She relies on the approval of her and her on the approval of him. Each silently killing each other, all the while believing they're pure. While the righteous silently endure. Running rampant, spreading discourse, no more unity and sanctification, just selfishness, abomination, infidelity and divorce. They've been convinced that evil is holy, but weren't told about damnation's matrimony. The evil prey on the good, while the good pray for the evil. Their hearts don't belong to God. The road they're traveling is wide and broad. No longer queens, but serpents, no longer kings but servants. They quote the scripture but don't believe the law. They curse God and the miracles they saw. They take credit in everything they do, they try to devour the Holy Spirit in you. Their fight is in vain. Thinking they can defeat God's children. It's insane. They throw their lies and try to pulls us down. They have no clue. They're souls are lost, damned, rebuked, never to be found. This race is won. We are protected, now run yourselves into the ground. We have the victory. We can't be defeated. Through The Messiah, God's lost have already been found.

satan is weak. God is strong. that's why he was so jealous. But God knew it all along and just like Him, we too are zealous. keep your tricks, we don't believe you. you and your lies get no respect. you can put down your fists and retreat to your corner, we've already won, we've seen your best. and it's not good enough, you just can't win, you lost before you tried, you ended before you could begin. yell until you pass out, scream

*Inspiration*

and cry and throw a fit, collect all your souls who were never my Father's, say your goodbyes because this is it. I rebuke you in the name of my Heavenly Father, the Holy Spirit, and my big brother who stole your sting. you have no dominion, get behind me, and let me show you what power really means.

## ***Confidence.***

One thing you can't argue with is confidence.

It doesn't need approval, acceptance, forgiveness or permission.

It stands alone.

Strong.

It is what it is.

It's like magical fairy dust…

You should sprinkle a little everywhere you go…

And leave a little on everything you do.

It's free!…

There's an unlimited supply.

If you want some all you have to do is ask.

The supplier gives it freely and willingly.

It's the purest drug.

Its benefits are love.

Better get you some.

Don't miss out on life without it.

*Inspiration*

Be bold

Be confident!

Be blessed!

Follow My Pen

## ***Bars.***

Silence is an A.R.T.ist's playground.

Silence.

The strongest voice in your life must be your God.

Listen.

There's never a better time than Now.

Time is the most powerful drug.

We're addicted to spending it. Time.

Love. Is. Everything.

I am. We are. More than a Conqueror.

Strength.

Courage.

Persistence.

Consistence.

Royalty.
((Inspired by Mali Music))

It's time out for ignorance, miseducation, and selfishness.

*Inspiration*

Turn off the world. And turn on your spirit.

Beauty.

Confidence.

Trust.

And Love.

## ***One.***

Instead of putting each other down OUR job is to lift each other up.

In prayer TWOgether WE stand, di-vided WE fall.

WE all are ONE.

Where one member of the body is weak, WE must be strong.

OUR purpose on this earth is to honor God and one another.

WE all have a responsibility, a gift, a role, and a purpose; to live, to serve and to love.

*Inspiration*

## ***Be***

Be the light
Be what's right
Be the standard
Be new
Be true
Be you
Be different
Be strong
Be yourself
Hold on
Be smart
Be smooth
Be quiet
Be cool
Be responsible
Be direct
Be careful
Be respect
Be watchful
Be ahead
Be a leader
Be led
Be obedient
Be the feel
Be the example
Be real!

## ***Pain…***

Pain is beautiful. It births passion. Concentration. Growth. Depth. Hearing. Sight. Focus. Silence. Determination. Courage. Cleansing.

Pain reveals purpose.

In times of pain you are vulnerable. Humble. Meek. Capable of being broken then built.

Pain strikes sensitivity to every emotion. Allowing you to be in tune with the inner depths of yourself. Uncovering the darkest places. The ones needing to be purified and renewed.

Pain allows the old self to be stripped away. It is the sleep needed during surgery, allowing the heart to be restored.

Embrace pain. It's the juice for growth. It is a sign of change and elevation. Contrary to the belief that it is weakness leaving the body, I believe it is strength being added to it.

*Inspiration*

## ***Wake Up!***

Your whole life, and mine are depending on you!

Who said being easy was great?

The lies…

Being great ain't easy!

If it were, everyone would be doing it…
It would be trendy… Like posting bible verses while smoking weed and being promiscuous.
It would lose its flavor and value if it were easily attained.

Greatness is mysterious and not yet completely defined.
It's a truth, a mental arrival and a spiritual awareness.

It ain't for everybody…

Greatness requires a continuous sacrifice, an intolerance for mediocrity and a hate for complacency.
A self-sacrifice and crucifixion of the flesh, daily.
And once you've removed the first layer, then another, and then another.

Each one of us encompasses the power to be as great as we dream to be.

If your dreams were unattainable, then how would our minds be able to envision them?

Greatness does not care where you started, or who you started with?

## Follow My Pen

What matters is where you finish!

When your story is complete will it be a waste of paper and time?

Your life depends on it, and so does mine!

There's no time to waste.

This life is so short!

There's work that is still to be done!

Did Jesus make excuses…

Did Noah give up…

Was Moses selfish…

Was Abraham weak…

NO!

Barriers must be removed!

Yokes must be broken!

Generational curses must end!

Wounds must be healed!

The lost must be found!

*Inspiration*

The darkness needs light!

It's time to bring morning to the night!

The tears must be dried!

The hungry must be fed!

The blind must be led!

Your future!

Their future!

My future!

Your future!

Depends on **you**!!!

### ***Prayer.***

Lord,

Please…

Replace pain with Peace
loss with Love
fear with Favor
ignorance with Intelligence
hatred with Humility
sin with Salvation
rituals with Relationship

Amen.

*Inspiration*

## **<u>U.N.I.</u>**

Together.

One.

Forever.

Become.

Discover.

Create.

Uncover.

Great.

Become.

Protect.

Shield.

Pray.

Heal.

Rise.

Emprise.

Advise.

Follow My Pen

Butterflies.

Fly.

Wise.

Skies.

Baptize.

Wait.

Fate.

Mate.

Above.

Pure.

Dove.

Greatest.

Love.

You.

Me.

We.

*Inspiration*

Just.

Us.

Forever.

Together.

Whatsoever.

U.

N.

I.

T.

Y.

♥

## *Poison...*

Don't do it!
Too many times, I...
Dumbed myself down for the comfort of the company of someone who was not mine...
Despite my better judgement, wisdom and knowledge I continued to seek, when hurt and emptiness was all I'd find...
If he is not willing to earn you, then my queen he does not deserve you...
Vacation this and designer that, it's all a waste of time... It will all eventually fade... You can't take it with you...
Your soul is what he will invest in, if his love is real and true...
My beloved, it takes much MUCH more...
If a big penis, muscles and a nice car is all he can offer then YOU, he can not afford...
What kind of *man* is willing to accept a paycheck without work... And my dear you are the highest of every prize...
It's sickening once your eyes have opened, but it's encouraging when you realize...
He is not a man if he finds himself worthy of what is God's... Especially if he does not even know Him...
Stop playing in the mud, getting your feathers dirty...
Gather up your pearls and stop giving them to the pigs...
Too many times, I...
Settled.
Was more afraid of being alone than being great...
Was too timid to be elevated, too selfish to offer the sacrifices needed, too immature to honor my value, too distracted to see my worth, too lazy to take a deeper look, and too stupid to perform the work it took...
If he can't pray with you, he can't stay with you... For true intimacy is in

*Inspiration*

communion with God… For in that time the depths of you are revealed…
How can he want your body without knowing your spirit… How can you be led by the blind…
The audacity of some to believe that you owe them your soul, when a price was paid for you, higher than the richest of silver and gold…
The speeches got old…
The behavior became unacceptable…
The stagnancy and complacency became uncomfortable…
It pushed me away… For I'm destined for greater, I am a child of God, the creator, you'll all see one day…
The nerve of those who believe that because of the money they make and the vacations they take, they are royalty…
Such a joke!
For the man that believes he can do it on his own is a dangerous and dying soul, and he'll take you with him… He may not know it but hell is his goal…
He is the walking dead…
Suicidal to your soul…
Run!
Let the ungodly be with the ungodly…
Ignore the whispers of those who do not see what you do…
Understand that only the spiritual eyes bestow the vision of what is true…
Be cautious of a man who has earthly idols, for he will always change…
For the wise and holy recognize that God is the only One who remains the same…
What he says, does and where he goes, is the makeup of who he is, sit

## Follow My Pen

back and reflect on him... Is he the one you really want to partner with in making your kids...

What is his destiny, is it everlasting... Is he reaching past worldly realms...

Is he concerned with your soul and where you'll spend eternity... is life with the creator his focus and goal...

And if so, what is he doing to get there... Is it all talk or superficial acts like the Romans back in the day...

Does he live by the truths of the bible, and the belief that Jesus is the ONLY way...

Keep walking past them all, leaving them where they stand...

Don't get distracted by the lies and the tries to prove to you that they are a godly man...

A real, Godly man, will never require you to step outside of your royal clothes...

Regardless of your age, race or financial classification, trust me, he knows...

Because he will love God first and keep God's will, he'll know the truth and he will obey...

He won't ask you to compromise your eternity for the temporary...

He won't tempt, influence or require you to disobey...

He will not contaminate his bride, ruin and stain her wedding dress...

For a man of God is obedient to His word, he'll desire to present you blameless...

Just be patient and be virtuous my love and you will see, that how he loves others is how he truly loves himself and all will align with God's plan accordingly.

*Inspiration*

## **<u>The Truth Is...</u>**

satan you're so wack!
Get a life!.. Oops I forgot, you can't!
I actually feel a little sorry for you.
The only friends you have are the ones you trick into liking you..
You have to pretend to be God just to get people to accept you..
How does it feel to forever be last place.
You actually have no power.
Congratulations, you've mastered the art of "smoke and mirrors.."
Your entire existence still gives glory to God, even though you hate Him..
You're an Idiot.
You hated Him because you wanted to be Him..
You only exist because of Him.
Didn't anyone tell you not to bite the hand that feeds you..
Now look at you.
You're miserable, and you desperately want company..
You're evil..
You're destitute..
You're pathetic..
Sometimes I feel a little sorry for you..
You'll always be a day late and a dollar short..
No matter what you do you'll always fail..
You're whole existence is like equality on the earth, you don't exist..
When my big brother returns you will reap all that you've sewn..
How does it feel…
Your time is limited, and you haven't used it wisely..
Tisk tisk
When I say His name you run…

## Follow My Pen

You're a coward…

Jesus!

LOL

You're just annoying..

You're like a gnat..

You can sometimes throw off my mood or agitate me.. but the truth of the matter is, you're just a bully..

You have no power..

You wish you could be me..

You're like a dog with no teeth that's mastered barking.


Get behind me!

*Inspiration*

## ***I can't wait!***

I heard about this type of love, but doubted that it could ever be…

In a world that taints love with pain, my vision was blurring and something this great was hard to see…

But there you were, standing strong and bold, filled firmly with the fire of Christ…

Without work, but simply by asking and believing God hand delivered you into my life…

Life's existence before you feels like it was all a dream, without question it's like you've always known me, you give life purpose and with love you teach me what love means…

When two souls are gathered as one with our Heavenly Father as our crown…

Everything before you does not exist, you are my love and my lord, to you I bow down…

You are amazingly beautiful, from the crown of your head to the soles of your feet…

I can't stop replaying it, over and over again, the day and the way that we would meet…

And just like that, now you're here and my life will never be the same…

I'm so full with love, I feel like my heart will explode… I want to share it with the world, I want the sky, the moon and trees to know your name…

I can't wait to share my life with you, I feel like it just began, every moment led up to this one and I will walk with you until the end…

I'm blessed to share this journey with someone so real and true…

Every lesson, every trial and every step led me directly to you…

You were made for me and I was made exactly for you… Now that I've tasted your sweet love, I'll never be the same… I don't know what else to do…

Except spend the rest of my life worshiping and rejoicing with the heavens in the unification of God's children…

A masterpiece that He has allowed you and I to be a part of, a symphony that He invited us to be instruments in…

I am honored to start this journey with my homie, my lover, and my friend…

I can't wait to call you my husband and for me to be your wife…

I can't wait to create this path, to paint this canvas that we call life…

*Inspiration*

I can't wait to start our lineage, to plant our family tree, to raise young men and women, warriors for Christ even stronger and wiser than you and me…

You're so beautiful. God is amazing. He is a God of His word. I didn't have to beg and plead, compromise or settle… Just like a gift, He gave us to each other in His impeccable and divine timing…

To those still waiting, don't be discouraged and don't give up, God's promises will be fulfilled….

He loves us deeply and wants the best for us, and in His timing His magnificence will be revealed….

He wants us to be happy, so just hold on and you will see, that there's someone made specially for you, just as He made my soulmate specially for me…

I can't wait to join our families and experience the moments that will build our history…

Some said that I was crazy, that someone like you would never be…

But look at us, we're here, God did it… Now let's allow His love, to be made perfect in us… For our marriage to be a ministry.

## *Questions...*

Why do you feed the monsters that make you feel inferior?

Why do you allow the same drug that is killing you make you feel alive?

It's all a lie.

Why do you entertain the lies that define you by your hips, lips and fingertips, when to measure yourself at that level is as equal as measuring dust to dirt?

Why do you love the system of materialism and depend on it to add value... when the very thing that devalues you is the love of material things?

Why give power to the evil and give evil to the powerless?

The media's very presence is to rob you of your joy, self-love, individuality and independence, and to be self-reliant on the opinion of others, the acceptance of someone else and the approval of those who have and will never *know* you.

These lies birth superficial occupations, causing some to spend their lives trying to "fit in" or "become"... Causing some to feel that they are not good enough, will never be enough, and result in them to taking their lives...

Who set this superficial standard?

Whose laws are we living by when we did not create ourselves?

What kind of system is set up to leave you broken and in debt?

Who developed this standard of "happiness" which only involves the characteristics of a drug addict?

Constantly needing and never content... Always wanting... Never satisfied.

And then the attitude of entitlement...

***"I don't care about your situation or circumstance, where you came from or how much you have or lack, I want more."***

A system that hates the sight of confidence, and is built to tear it down.

A system that tell us to find a problem, criticize and ridicule someone when they are trying their best. To prey on the weak to hide your own weaknesses.

A system that says, "No matter what you do you will never be good enough..."

Why do we feed this monster?

What happened to uniqueness, beauty, and creativity, that aren't at the expense of someone's loss for another man's gain?

What happened to caring and sharing?

What happened to a place of peace and not so much need and greed?

## Follow My Pen

What happened to a standard of self-respect and not neglect?

When did we give up?

When did we give in?

When did we decide?

Haven't you realized yet that we have the power?

We control this space.

We can make the changes.

We are in control.

But do we want to do better?

Much like a drug addict our dependency has grown too strong.

Our level of acceptance has gotten to high.

We think we're God, but we don't have a clue…

But we don't want to stand out. We don't want to be challenged. When the fire gets too hot we want to run.

Where are the fighters?

Where are the soldiers?

*Inspiration*

Who is willing to lose everything they thought they knew to find what is true?

Follow My Pen

## *L...O...V...E...*

So I write...

What do you do when a love as equivalent as your own stares you right in the face...

With a boldness and strength that you fear could actually overtake you...

A love that looks into the depths of your soul and tells you that there is nothing to fear...

The sweetness of a love that fills your body and elevates your mind...

That you get lost in, and not only lose but disregard all sense of time...

A love that is pure and unashamed to show it's all...

That answers all of your questions and leaves you with no doubts...

Left with nothing but the silence of its sweet fragrance...

A love so pure and clean that leaves no sorrow beneath it...

An untainted, educated, intelligent, beautiful, easy, sweet, joyous, love...

A glimpse of God in every thought, that must be from up above...

What is this love?...

Could it be everything I've always dreamt it would be?...

*Inspiration*

Although I always believed it could happen, a part of me doubted I would ever see...

Love...

Pure, bright, light, heavy, love.

## ***Who are you?...***

Would you still exist if no one was watching?...

Is the question I ask in a day and time where social media acceptance dictates, and influences the minds of the masses, and directs their life decisions.

How many of you found yourselves wanting to take more vacations just because of the people you follow on social media?... Or, how many of you find that your taste in music, television shows, current events, and latest fashion all stem from social media in some way?...

It is interesting how inauthentic and less individualistic we have become due to a tool that has actually brought us closer together...

Is it a gift and a curse?... Well that depends on how it's used. Unlike before where you wouldn't know what your childhood friends were up to until your class reunions, now you can check in and even communicate with them whenever they cross your mind, with just a couple clicks of a button or taps to a screen.

Has this tool desensitized us, are we less equipped for the mysteries of getting to know one another, patience, and has it handicapped us to the art of conversation? Are we more fascinated by those that we can't see, touch or talk to, and less concerned by those that we actually can?...

Is it possible that we have slowly but surely allowed computers to actually think for us, completely?... I believe so.

*Inspiration*

It is not until you step away from social media that you realize just how much time you actually spend using it. It is also very intriguing what you can come up with on your own when you do not allow any outside influence to shape your ideas of beauty, fashion, health, love or living.

I feel sorry for the books, and the authors, a little bit, because since the rise of the "social media empire" people's minds are less capable of focusing for extended periods of time… I mean what do you expect when you are used to viewing constant flashes of a variety of different types of news and media, updated every second?

In my opinion, social media, like anything else can be beneficial as long as it is not abused.

This is so important because what happens to us all when we are drowned in our inability to think?

It starts small. It feels good. But like any drug, it will eventually kill you, or incapacitate you in some way.

I would challenge every person who uses it to take a break, let's say for 21 days (spiritually and scientifically proven to be the time it takes to break a habit); to allow your brains to refocus and rebuild; find out what life is like without it, and if you have developed a severe dependence on it to function…

The results should be interesting.

The goal and purpose of these thought evoking questions are to spark self-reflection and evaluation, in hopes to regain individuality and creativity in a mundane world. So many people have become good at doing the exact same things: keeping "their world" updated on the most current status of their life while pretending they could care less about public opinion; believing they are different by participating in the social media nation "slightly differently" than those in their social circles; and last but not least, using social media to change the way people view social media…

Best wishes!

*Inspiration*

## **<u>She.</u>**

I'm in a lifelong committed relationship with someone special, and I am so in love!

She is kind, sweet, caring, loving, giving, passionate, humorous, glamorous, dramatic, talented, spontaneous, intelligent, God-fearing, cool, and ambitious!

When I look at her she makes me smile.

I am proud of her.

We have so much fun together.

She is beautiful inside and out.

We spend quality time together.

She is unique and creative.

I have watched her grow.

As she grows, I grow.

I appreciate every stage and season of her life.

She is my best friend.

We tell each other everything.

She never lets me down.

## Follow My Pen

She lifts me up when I am down.

She reminds me that everything will be ok.

She motivates me to be the best and never ever settle for less.

She is honest with me, no matter what.

She always has my back.

When I don't have anyone else, she is *always* there.

No matter how many times I've hurt her she does not keep score.

She is optimistic.

She is a wanderer, a thinker and a dreamer.

She is intrigued by the objects *outside* of the box.

She is always striving to become better.

She wants to break the molds and defy the odds.

She desires to set a new standard.

She is an encourager and a life-giver.

Her words are like sweet fruit.

When everyone else goes right she walks left.

*Inspiration*

She has no desire to "fit in."

She was made to stand out.

She constantly reminds me of the treasures I hold within.

She's closer to me than the closest friend.

I love the times when it is just she and I.

There are no needs for barriers and guards.

She is at her best when she is just being herself.

I am the most comfortable in her presence.

I enjoy the sound of her voice.

She always self-reflects.

She never judges.

Her heart is the size of the universe.

Her soul is deeper than the oceans.

Sometimes the magnitude of her potential frightens me.

She likes the *road less traveled*.

Her time is precious.

### Follow My Pen

I will not share her with just anybody.

She speaks from the heart.

She lives through her heart.

She sees from her spirit.

She gives from her soul.

She is honest.

She is confident.

She is graceful.

She is strong.

She is fearless.

She is bold.

*She is **me**.*

**This is dedicated to everyone who has loved, is loving and longs for love. The greatest love was already given to each and every one of us before we were even born. We spend our entire existence tapping into that love, getting to know that love, and giving that love to one another. Live, learn and love yourself, and then loving everyone else will feel no different. Just as you've made bad decisions, let yourself down, and**

***hurt yourself… for that, you will understand, and accept and love everyone else.***

Love yourself.

## ***Endurance***

### Peace and Hope

"Therefore, since we have been justified through faith, we have peace with God through our Lord Jesus Christ, through whom we have gained access by faith into this grace in which we now stand. And we boast in the hope of the glory of God. Not only so, but we also glory in our sufferings, because we know that suffering produces perseverance; perseverance produces character; and character produces hope. And hope does not put us to shame, because God's love has been poured out into our hearts through the Holy Spirit, who has been given to us."

Romans 5:1-5

Inspiration

## *Spiritual*

One of the intricacies of being an open book is that while giving off light and life you often are open to darkness...

As a writer, and as a person, I find myself always having to "prove" myself to people... It's as if they believe they have already "arrived," or... they see something in me that draws out their curiosities about themselves... It makes them question themselves and in turn question me... Sometimes my biggest struggle is not allowing this to wear me down or discourage me towards the human race, but to not take it personal and to remember and focus on what this exchange is truly about...

I am and always have been open, it is not something I struggle with or had to create, it has always just been me. Because of this, I face a different struggle internally... People dish and take what they lack and want because during our encounters there are no walls to climb or knock down... It's a spiritual struggle, even with those I am close to... I find myself talking to my spirit nonstop, always evaluating, discussing and digging to find the questions and answers as to what these exchanges mean...

A lot of times I am faced with people's deepest and darkest insecurities, disguised as jokes, smiles and meaningless conversations... Remember from the abundance of the heart the mouth speaks... *(Luke 6:45)* It's never a big secret or mystery as to *what* they are saying... My concern usually lies in *why* they are saying it... Call it a gift and a curse... It's hard to constantly have to physically, mentally, and spiritually prepare yourself every time you walk into a room... Being around loved ones and close friends sometimes lightens the load, but even with them, you're sometimes faced with whatever spirit they're currently carrying, it's like always working your body, soul and spirit, all while trying to keep yourself together, 24 hours a day, 7 days a week, with the exception of sleep, when you're not still dreaming about these things…

This is why I am so comfortable being alone, and in silence, only surrounded by my own thoughts… Dealing with everyone else's demons has helped me to easily deal with my own… This is why I am comfortable in my own skin, not easily frightened and rarely intimidated… Not much shocks me, because often times I've already seen the characteristics before the play from a person… The more layers a person puts on the more they are trying to hide… But, don't get me wrong, sometimes my own spirit can be too hard to bear… And this is when the meaning of the spiritual exchange fulfills its purpose…

Because I am so used to dealing with these things internally, on my own, it is extremely difficult for me to ask for help… I internalize a lot of what I feel and need… But every so often someone can pick up on my spirit and lends a helping hand, or a word of encouragement along the way… And this gives me the strength to continue on… facing, battling and healing spirits…

These transfers of spirits allows me to see people's hearts, their wounds, their hurts, their fears and their strengths… It has allowed me to love openly and purely, without fear… I am not afraid. After seeing past clothes, physicality and words, you tend to look at life and everything in it differently… most people will never fully understand… This has given me strength and courage… Not to fight one another, this war is spiritual *(Ephesians 6:12-13)*, and sometimes it is not necessarily a fight, but a need, a cry for help, the sick wanting to be healed… This is what it is all about… This is what the Holy Spirit is for… This is what gives us a direct connection to God's power… this is His gift to us… This is what makes us children of The Most High God…

Past the fleshly shell, and the worthless clothes, and empty words… This is spiritual . . .

Follow My Pen

### ***Your Soul is My Goal…***

I want to read your mind

But that process will take time

I enjoy the seek

The rewards I find

The longer I search

The higher I climb

The deeper I go

The journey is mine

There is no math to calculate this path

There is no need for fear or doubt

Reading the map of your mind that unveils the tunnels to your heart is what I'm about

Where your core is exposed and your spirit illuminates

He who masters is the one who waits

The soul is the goal

*In everything, I love.*

*Inspiration*

## ***How Jesus looks to me…***

All of the colors of the rainbow,

All of the depths of the sea,

All of the sounds of the wind,

All of the heights of the trees,

All of the dreams of a child,

All of the mysteries of the mountains,

All of the sounds of the wild,

All of the purity of the fountains,

All of the lengths of the desserts,

All of the shades of the skies,

All of the time of the past,

All of the scents of the flowers,

All of the seconds, minutes and hours,

All of the different languages and people,

All of the planets and the nations,

All of the magical wonders,

Everything in God's creation.

When I stop and look around, it's everything that I see,

Everything that is beautiful, pure and sweet,

That's how Jesus looks to me!

*"Falling in love with Jesus, is the best thing I've ever, ever done!"*

*Inspiration*

## ***<u>Peace.</u>***

Peacefully, when I cried, You rocked me to sleep,

Peacefully, when I was weak, You carried me,

Peacefully, when the silence became too loud, You sang songs of joy to my heart,

Peacefully, Your love brought me close, now I never want to be a part,

Peacefully, You loved me, without a price, now I cannot imagine a day, without you in my life,

Peacefully, You cared for me, when I did not care for myself,

Peacefully, through everyone and everything, You have been my help,

Peacefully, with the darts of the devil, You have been my shield,

Peacefully, throughout this war, You never left me, You stood with me on the battle field,

Peacefully, you have set my eyes, my heart, and sights on what's above,

Peacefully, you've taught me, the true meaning of love,

Peacefully, you've revealed your heart and shown me the true depths of a friend,

Peacefully, you'll never leave me, You are with me until the end,

Peacefully, I have been adopted, into your Holy kingdom I now belong,

Peacefully, I've experienced that your love has no end, it goes on, and on, and on,

Peacefully, your power gave me strength, my weakness made you strong,

Peacefully, through all trials and tribulations, your wisdom gave me strength and spiritual elevation,

Peacefully, you're transforming me and taking me to a higher place,

Peacefully, you are molding me, and shaping me with grace,

Peacefully, I thank you, for the crown of humility on my head you have placed,

For I know that this is the first step to the steps of following Christ,

Peacefully I know and understand that this is the journey to giving up my life.

Thank you Jesus, my best friend, my brother, my savior, my lover.

*He says, "Be still, and know that I am God; I will be exalted among the nations, I will be exalted in the earth."*

***Psalms 46:10***

*Inspiration*

## ***Lessons of Love…***

He, taught me…
the beginning of love, in a way I had never experienced,
The door to my curiosity had now been opened,
Both innocent, young and fresh, without a clue of the confusion that lied ahead,
Only if we'd saved ourselves from this mess…
Confusion, thoughts, heart-aches, all tampering the purity of our minds,
all for a feeling we were desperate to find,
Here I gained the basic tools needed to fight, create, and maneuver through this journey called love…

    He, taught me…
    the first lesson of love,
    What you release just rests up above, later to fall right back down,
    like raindrops on your ground.
    Love is a mirror, reflecting exactly who you are,
    What you see is exactly what you get,
    So mistakes I made, and his heart I played,
    immature and with regret.

        He, taught me…
        an entirely new existence of love, never had I ever loved someone as purely as the white of a dove,
        I gave freely, openly and true, there was nothing I would not do,
        Dangerously in love but not afraid of what lied ahead,
        Blinded, we created an angel from a sinful bed,

But this love was tearing me down, trying to elevate but still on the ground,
Little did I know then, I would learn everything else I'd ever need to know,
but of course I had to move on because I desired to grow.

      He, taught me…
the depths, shapes and faces of love,
Due to my past, this time I had a plan and a goal,
He was different, a difficult and confused soul,
But for some reason I was drawn in from the start, sucked in and enticed, from "What's up?" he had my heart…
So no matter how hard his love was to gain, I fought for him until my heart was drained,
But little did I know, just how much I would grow, from this dramatic love show,
Our story was far from over, we both just could not see,
But competitively, he pushed me into being the best that I could possibly be…

      He, taught me…
to love patiently, purely and careful,
He gained my attention because of a persistence I'd never felt,
He patiently knocked at the door until I gracefully handed him the keys,

*Inspiration*

I thought that at this point we had arrived, little did I know I would barely survive...
Where I was finished he was just getting started,
I had no clue the maze he would put me through,
Trying so hard to be what I needed him to,
Trying to be all that he could be, but all the while he was fooling himself and me,
He could not be what was best for me, when he didn't even know who he, was...
He was lost and tried to find himself in me,
We fought a losing battle from two different worlds, resulting in the tragic change of an innocent girl.

> My love became tainted and selfish,
> the purity of my heart was filled with something else,
> Feeling owed I wanted what was mine,
> It was not an option for me this time,

> I viscously went after love,
> with a vengeance I went after
> what I thought I wanted,
> forgetting the lessons of the
> past, on a search for something
> that would last…

And so I landed in the line of sight of one wrong whom I wanted to be so right…

> He, taught me…
> to always be myself,
> to let go and let love…
> Without regard to my
> truths, I digressed to the
> mentality of my youth, I
> began to let go, and just
> let life flow,
> but eventually
> something would have
> to give, someone would
> have to go,
> I fought a battle
> between myself and the
> power up above,
> I gave in and gave up
> and allowed what I
> thought was love,
> to run its course,

*Inspiration*

Although I knew it wasn't right I kept tapping into love as my source,
He was draining me, but I kept going, despite the warning signs his spirit kept showing,
No matter what happened I still gave my best,
I'd entered a battle between spirit and man, despite our attempts my soul had no rest, I began to realize this love was a test,
A testament of who I loved more,
so despite the outer beauty of this union I had to walk out the door,

It was God, He was calling me, He was tired of waiting,
He wanted my all, He would not let go, so my name He continued to call,
I'd never experienced a strength such as His, He would not let go, He was setting me free, for He saw and knew all and was the true lover of my destiny,

my soul was uneasy, I could not get rest, He wanted my everything, He fought for my best,

So I laid down my weapons, I gave up the fight, I knew He would come, like a thief in the night,

I had to be ready, I wanted to be His, and He to be mine, He was saving my life,

He nursed my sick body, mended my heart and stayed by my side, He was getting me ready, His beloved, His beautiful bride,

so everything I would give,

because without him there's no way I would live,

He was there all along, He helped me survive, because of Him I made it, my heart is alive,

Some called me crazy, some even laughed, but none have a clue what I experienced in the past,

The love that taught me patience, would put my journey to an end, as he left me not as a fighter, or a lover, but as a friend,

He taught me longevity, and persistence of the heart, we remained so close, despite how long and far we were apart,

He gave meaning to the journey, and taught me that life is so short, and through a tragedy, life is what you make it, you must train and compete in life, just like a sport,

I gained an appreciation, and learned to never take love for granted, I learned that growth is produced through nurture, time and love, I learned that pride will imprison you from what you want, and that fear will trap you into what you don't.

*Inspiration*

My heart has been pulled, pricked, cut, ripped, reshaped, drained, filled, sliced, juggled, shaken, stolen, gambled, borrowed, stirred, punched, stomped, punctured, and played from mistreat… But it still beats…

The beauty of it all, is that I've taken it with grace, it has allowed me to elevate to a new and higher place,
a place of understanding, patience and truth, a place of rejuvenation, a rejuvenation, a new heart of youth,
I have been reborn, with a new attitude, a new behavior, I have been clothed in righteousness, all glory to my King and Savior, there's no place I'd rather be than in His eminent favor,

I now know what love is and that there are no mistakes, when the heart purely, truly and fully gives it can never be replaced,
So to those that helped me, along the way, I just want to say thank you, because without you, I wouldn't be where I am and where I am going today!

God bless!

## *Gut Check*

Look in the mirror…

What do you see?…

Is it the girl in the magazine, or on the t.v.?…

Is is the guy that you're dating, or the girl you call "best friend?"…

Is it your mother, your father, or who you long to be in the end?…

Who have you become, if you met God would it be you that He would know?…

What is the content of your character, is truth in your heart or just what you show?…

Are you comfortable in the silence, are you ok with being alone?…

Do your own thoughts bore you, who are you when everyone is gone?…

What do you stand on, what is your desire?…

Do you change with the wind?…

Are you confused and constantly compromising your righteousness with sin?…

Have you allowed God to examine you, can you say that your heart is pure?…

Are you tainted and don't even know it, are you secretly insecure?…

*Inspiration*

Where are you headed, is it to the left or to the right?...

Or are you headed in whichever direction in is currently in your line-of-sight?...

Who are you listening to, is it your spirit, your heart, your mind, or your soul?...

Is allowing the Father to be your one and only guidance, your truth, it that really your goal?...

A lot of people have mastered the "look" of being righteous and perfected the illusion of being whole...

But it's in those quiet times, those isolations, those moments when your soul can't rest...

Half the battle is completely quieting distractions, and I personally can attest?...

That when you silence every voice but God's you will finally be at your best...

You can read a million books and adapt to every trend, but who you really are can only be found within...

Your true spiritual elevation is solely your work of art, you can either fit in and blend in, or truly be set apart...

## Follow My Pen

It's not enough to just go through the motion and proclaim to be Holy in your youth, just remember God sees and knows all, He searches the heart for spirit and truth…

It's time to grow up and stand on your own, don't be afraid to be alone, because you're not alone…

Your gut is your core, it's the center of your strength…

So who is at your center, is it truly you or everyone you come in contact with…

Make God your core that is His place and NO ONE or NOTHING else… From here no matter what is taken away or who leaves, you know you're not by yourself…

God is here, He is enough, His love is all you need, let him pluck the dying roots of this world and plant and everlasting seed…

Satan is like a vampire, he is constantly at your neck… he wants to steal, kill, and destroy…

So get your mind right, this is your gut check!

*Inspiration*

## ***The Beauty of the Battle***

It is indeed in times of pressure that you gain your poise,
In times of desperation you discover your determination,
In times of hardships you discover your help,
In times of loss you see gain,
In times of weakness you learn your strength,
In pain there is purpose,
In fire there is purification,
In isolation there is growth,
In the silence there is music,
In times of feeling lost there is actually direction,
In blindness there is guidance,
In persecution there is peace,
In tearing down there is building,

We have the choice to either allow life to make us bitter or better.

God's ways are the total opposite of our own.

When we proclaim to be His children and times of adversity arise we have to understand who and whose we are.

Nothing is by chance or coincidence, but in the perfecting of our spirits to be made more like Christ.

Because our flesh is selfish and born to die, God is constantly peeling away at the layers that separate us from Him.

This is the beautification process.

*"For we are not fighting against flesh-and-blood enemies, but against evil rulers and authorities of the unseen world, against mighty powers in this dark world, and against evil spirits in the heavenly places."*

**Ephesians 6:12**

*Inspiration*

## ***War of Words...***

This has been a topic that has rested on my mind for almost an entire year. I could not articulate what I was feeling exactly until today... So here it is.

We live in a day and time where self-expression is at an all-time high. Prudence and meekness have been traded in for ignorance and selfishness. I say that because we no longer care or value the feelings of our neighbor, it is all about us... and how we feel. Now more than ever, I understand why God advised us to be careful with our words and to love one another. Because what you release is what you receive. You cannot speak harshly toward someone without have anger in your own heart...

*"You brood of snakes! How could evil men like you speak what is good and right? For whatever is in your heart determines what you say."*

**Matthew 12:34**

You cannot be selfish in your endeavors and intents without feeling as though you are in need, and wanting everything for yourself. One who truly cares and gives freely and whole-heartedly, putting their neighbor before themselves, is the richest of all men and holds the happiness and joy of the Holy Spirit. There is no other way.

So often I hear people so quickly get angry and frustrated with each other without realizing that we are one, so if you do not have "time" for your neighbor, then don't be surprised if God does not have "time" for you... You have to be what you want to see! That is the only way.

*"A good man brings good things out of the good stored up in his heart, and an evil man brings evil things out of the evil stored up in his heart. For the mouth speaks what the heart is full of."*

**Luke 6:45**

We are spiritual beings with power. Our words manifest and bring life, whether that be good life or bad life. Today my *Our Daily Bread* reading discussed the war between Serbia and Austria-Hungary which resulted in World War I. This historical tragedy was compared to the war we fight daily with our words. The effects of our words are stronger than that of guns and violence. Proverbs 15:1 says, *"A soft answer turns away wrath, but a harsh word stirs up anger."* How many times have we revisited a situation and realized that it just was not that serious. The energy and time we put into the most meaningless moments rob us of the joy and heart-felt lessons that we can learn in times where, if we just put others before ourselves and truly love them as we love ourselves, are priceless.

*"All things are lawful, but not all things are profitable. All things are lawful, but not all things edify."*

**1 Corinthians 10:23**

The "game" of words stems from pride and is an immaturity that will forever imprison you from what you truly want. Be wise… The bible talks about when Jesus was being crucified and how despite how, *"He was oppressed and He was afflicted, yet He opened not His mouth,"* Isaiah 53:7. Here we are not experiencing half of the oppression as Jesus did but yet we go out and look for battles by not holding out tongues, causing wars in our own lives that could have completely been omitted.

Proverbs, one of my favorite books in the bible, oozing with wisdom states,

*"A wholesome tongue is a tree of life... and a word spoken in due season, how good it is."*

**Proverbs 15:4,23**

The next time you are faced with a situation that makes you want to "keep it real" ask yourself is it necessary for uplifting to the body of Christ?... *"What would Jesus do?"* Will these words bring life or break down my neighbor?... What will these words reflect of me and what is on the inside of *my* heart?... Remember that what you deflect is what you truly reflect. This battle is mainly personal as well as spiritual, so there is no need to try to break one another down.

*A careless word may kindle strife,*
*A cruel word may wreck a life:*
*A timely word may lessen stress,*
*A loving word may heal and bless.* -AU

**Prayer:** *"Lord, make me an instrument of your peace. Where there is hatred, let me sew love."*

Because you choose the high road, it doesn't make you "weak," it not only reveals your strength but plants a seed of strength into someone else. Choose your words and your battle carefully!

*"A soft answer turns away wrath, but a hard word stirs up anger."*

**Proverbs 15:1**

Becoming better is a decision and an action that only **YOU** can make!!!

Be blessed!

## *What are we fighting for?...*

I've recently been faced with a number of situations that have forced me to look at the world through a new set of eyes. The more I journey as a disciple, the more I realize that the way our world is set up, and the way we are taught growing up is exactly the opposite of how God views us. Author Philip Yancey writes, *"To gain a new perspective, look at the world upside down as Jesus did..."* I found this very interesting because I always measure what is "right" by comparing it to love, through God's definition and instruction. I've realized that in order to follow in the footsteps of Christ we have to go to the places no one else wants to go, do the things that no one else want to do, and be the things that everyone else are afraid to be... Matthew 9:12 states, *"Those who are well have no need of a physician, but those who are sick..."* This is extremely important because we are always taught to chase after the highest and the richest, but what about those that are without... Wouldn't it make more sense to partner with those who need help, in order to be great and prosper... Or why abandon the poor and sick to join with the rich, when all that does is leave the poor, poor... How is that solving any problem?... Jesus came to do the dirty work that everyone else was afraid to do... And when it comes to love, which we know is the most important entity in God's eyes, we have to take time and invest in the ones that are lacking. They are looking for love in all of the wrong places, and we as believers but be "the way, the truth and the life..." John 14:6. We cannot give up on those that need us most, we have to pray and fast, interceding on behalf of them... We have to fight! No, it is not/will not be easy but it has to be done. What if half way along Jesus' journey He gave up and quit... Where would we be? All of humanity would be damned! So we must pattern ourselves after the One and great, true leader, and fight this Holy war. He has already completed the hardest

part of this battle, and we already know the outcome, which should fuel our fire to stand in the gap for those that need a little more healing, a little more car and a little more love. For several years I have had to deal with those that are trying to find their way, and I always asked God "why?" Now I know! It is because they see the light of our Lord in me and they are drawn to it, God's word will never fail. He instructs us to just do His will, obey His word and follow the footsteps of Christ, and our light, through the Holy Spirit, will do the rest... Save souls! Praise God, because He could have chosen anyone else... He could have wiped out all of humanity and started over... He can receive praise from the angels, and even the trees... But he chose you and me!

Glory be to The Most High God!!!

*"We know, Jesus, that You sought the lowly ones who were rejected by others. We want to be like You. Open our eyes and show us how. We long to be used by You to bless others."*

***-Jonathan L. Aaron***

*Inspiration*

## ***Repentance***

Repentance is God-given…

You have already been forgiven…

Now pick up your cross and continue to follow me…

There's work to do.

*"And because of his glory and excellence, he has given us great and precious promises. These are the promises that enable you to share his divine nature and escape the world's corruption caused by human desires.*

*In view of all this, make every effort to respond to God's promises. Supplement your faith with a generous provision of moral excellence, and moral excellence with knowledge, and knowledge with self-control, and self-control with patient endurance, and patient endurance with godliness, and godliness with brotherly affection, and brotherly affection with love for everyone.*

*The more you grow like this, the more productive and useful you will be in your knowledge of our Lord Jesus Christ."*

***2 Peter 1:4-8 New Living Translation (NLT)***

## ***Time***

I'ma need that back!

That attention you demanded and I so graciously gave…

That time I gave, becoming a captain, trying to save…

I saved, put on a cape and gave, gave my time, brought you in and made you mine…

Made you mine and changed your mind…

I changed your mind, but not your ways, your ways were the only thing that couldn't stay… That could've saved…

You could've saved us, we did not have to end…

But it was bound to end the minute we tried to begin…

To begin, I had to convince… Myself to proceed despite the depths of my need…

My need was deeper than you could see, but you planted a seed…

A seed that began to grow, and my love started to show, how in the world were we to know…

Well, maybe "we" weren't to know, but I was well aware… but instead of making a move I continued to stare…

Staring at the future knowing it quickly was going to become my past…

Because of my past I was well aware that this love affair was not going to last…

This time would be my last… I was to blame, to blame because I knew better…

But in fear I refused to do better… So I continued to travel down the same dusty road…

This road only continued to compromise my soul… This vicious cycle quickly got old…

These lies got old… Your tries got old…

Old…

I outgrew… And you knew… You knew but your battle was similar to mine…

Wanting to be mine but wasting your time… Knowing we were committing a crime…

The crime of killing time…

How many times do we kill our own time…

The most precious gift of all time…

Man has searched but been unsuccessful every time… In their pursuit to define, to refine, to slow down, and to take… Time.

So,

For the attention, mind, love, soul, and time… And all that was mine…

I'ma need that back!

*Inspiration*

## ***From males to Men...***

Pardon me if your hello, did not open the window to my soul,
It will take more than a text, "Hey" or "What's up" to peel back the layers of this fruit.

This flower takes time to blossom and bloom,
You are one of several silently fighting for my attention in the room.

There are no guards or fears, just wisdom and patience,
Nothing permanent will be obtained through lust, mediocrity will not produce greatness.

Where have the roles been reversed?
Why do men feel that they are the prize?

When God clearly laid out the instructions right before our eyes.

I will not give my all to the deception that you call, love.

There's only one who deserves that, look up… His presence is above.

To Him I am the prize, and to me it is He… If your leadership isn't the Father, the Son and the Holy Ghost how could we ever be.

If you're listening to the world and I am listening to the Son, it is physically, mentally and spiritually impossible to ever fully become, one.

Eve was made from man, so indeed men are great, but to manipulate and degrade your own rib shows that it's truly yourself that you hate…

# Follow My Pen

Excuse me if I am not hypnotized by your lies,
I am awake and alive and I realize,
That it takes more than a smile, a nice build or money in the bank,

Oh no, don't shut down, run, or shy away, it's my job to be frank.

This will take more, much, much more and with God I will continuously elevate,
It will take a man, a man of God to even begin to comprehend the scent of my soul that will captivate.

This level is incomprehensible to most, and unrecognizable to some,
What I am saying is that if God is not the head of your life please do not even approach.

I can do without the meaningless conversations, I do not crave the presence of the emptiness you embody… You see, I am complete so whoever God sends to me will only compliment me.

Try to grasp that I could care less about the number in your account, or the designer you are enslaved to, none of that amounts, to the higher calling I have been engraved to, become.

My Lord is the only One.

Let me tell you what example of a man I have been given… A man who walked this filthy earth sinless and blameless so that my sins could be forgiven.

*Inspiration*

A man who dedicated his life solely to win the souls that have been lost… A man who gave up his own life to pay the ultimate cost.

A man who delivered salvation to me on a silver platter, One who loves me more than I love myself, One who promised me that my flaws don't even matter.

He handed me His love, without asking me to earn it, freely, given, and to know Him is to know love, you better learn it…

Because between he and I, the world is a stepping stone to a higher place of majesty and splendor.

So if while I am here you cannot add to this then we have nothing to discuss.

As of matter of fact, your attempts to map out a plan on your own only brings me deeper disgust.

There is nothing you can do for me if you are not being led by The One and Only.

I am not trying to be rude but we are speaking two different languages so please don't even bother.

I am striving for holiness and you for pleasure, your goals are feeble and mine are strong,

I am tired of playing with peasants, no we cannot be friends because we do not really get along.

## Follow My Pen

I will not dumb down and you will not rise up, so I must depart and preserve my precious time…

You have no entitlement to what is God's, he died for me, so what can you offer for what is His and what is mine?…

How can we form a trinity when you are unaware of your identity?

Stop making deception, lust and idleness your wives, I am trying to save our lives…

It is time, take your place, the disconnect is between man and God.

Order will not be regained until this bond has been restored.

Detox the estrogen and replenish your manhood, it's time out for laziness, excuses and complacency…

Focused on the wrong things while doing just enough to get by… My attempt is only one but I will spend my life giving this one thing a try.

No I am not perfect, and I have yet to arrive. I crave correction, but only from those who are led by my Father, and that is for my protection.

I strive to awaken your greatness, because He created me as your help.

You are not alone, none of us can do this by ourselves…

Get your souls, hearts and minds right, your creator is returning like a thief in the night…

*Inspiration*

So, I will not settle, I will not give up, I will not give in, I will fight until the end, I will continue to try…

We're in a spiritual battle and this is my war cry.

Follow My Pen

## ***My Angel***

My angel . . .

Plays on the rays of the sun

While holding hands with the son

Watching me and waiting patiently

Bestowing the knowledge our hearts yearn to know

Watching me grow

Singing the songs of the sky

Whispering when I cry

Laughing with the angels

Dancing with the rain

Blowing away the pain

To him it all makes sense

He is protected by truth

Surrounded by youth

He is love

And love is he

*Inspiration*

They are me

We.

My love child. My angel.

## ***Love Child***

I am a child of love . . .

There's no wonder why I love so much . . .

I love so hard . . .

I love so tough . . .

Love is my drug . . .

I can't breathe, can't eat, can't think, can't see, can't sleep, without it . . .

It drives me . . .

It thrives me . . .

It moves me . . .

It uses me . . .

It is me, and I am it . . .

Love.

I am bound to love . . .

I am grounded by love . . .

I am indebted to love . . .

Because love made me.

*Inspiration*

I am nothing without love . . .

And love is nothing without me . . .

Love is everything . . .

It is all around me . . .

It's in my highs, my lows, my ups, my downs, and my round and rounds . . .

I am wrapped up . . .

Caught up . . .

Brought up . . .

In love!

Follow My Pen

## ***Black Men.***

It's not about your height

Your strength or your might

It's not about your account

Clothes, cars, shoes, homes, amounts

It's not about your status

Despite our accomplishments you see the way they look at us

It's not about your job, career or social class

It's not in your pecks, your biceps or your abs

It's about your light, your mind and your right

It's in your character, your integrity and your love

It's about the relationship, the mysterious connectivity with The Creator up above

It's about the covenant and the fact that He made you first

It's about your destiny, your mission, your right that was given at birth

It's about defeating the evil, not allowing the enemy to tear you down

It's about keeping your head up, and trusting that your help meet is always around

*Inspiration*

It's about that reconciliation, that divine sealing that is true

It's about the whisper, that **je ne sais quoi** from inside of you

It's about knowing, who you are and from where you came

It's about loving, no longer discrediting those that are the same

It's about facing, no longer tearing down the outside to match the inner

It's about losing your old self to find the true winner

It's about building, restructuring and recalculating the math

It's about taking the first step to lead generation upon generation on a new path

It's about your heart, your soul, your spirit, getting rid of the old and embracing the new, the true

These are the reasons that I love you.

## *Elevation = Separation*

When God speaks the entire universe listens. God created an order and just as He spoke day and night into existence, He spoke an order and direction for our lives to fulfill a greater purpose. Sometimes in order to complete a task we must isolate ourselves and allow God's voice to manifest. We have to remove all distractions and hindrances. If we aren't sure what they are or how to eliminate them God will surely do it for us. Remember that no great task was completed over night. Even God took 7 days to create our being, existence and universe. Although sometimes the road seems endless and there is no light in sight, remember that when you can't see your way, or how to make it another day, that God is working His hardest. When you are overcome by your circumstances and can't find your way out, close your eyes, grab His hand and let Him lead you. When you are tired, your strength is gone and you can't go on, let Him carry you. No great story has come without a great journey and sacrifice. Jonah spent three days and three nights in the belly of a whale to come out a humble and obedient servant. **Matthew 12:40** Noah was 500 years old when God instructed him to take on the journey of the covenant, the construction of the ark to forever restart mankind. **Genesis 5:32** Moses stayed on Mount Sinai for 40 days and 40 nights communing with God to later provide generation upon generations with God's sacred instructions to man. **Exodus 34:28** Joseph was imprisoned for 11 years before becoming king. **Genesis 39, 41** In the course of approximately a couple months to 1-year Job lost everything he owned, including family, servants, possessions and his own health, **Job 30:16, 42:12-13** to later gain it back and more, and become "the model for endurance and perseverance." **James 5:11** Abraham and Sarah waited 25 years for God's promise of a child, Isaac. **Genesis 18:14** Jacob waited and served for 7 years so that he could marry Rachel. **Genesis 29:20** And the greatest of them all, Jesus, spent 40 days and 40 nights in the wilderness, fasting and praying, with no food and no home, to take on every temptation as a living sacrifice for His fellow man. **Luke 4:2** We now can see that great purpose is birthed from great persecution. Don't fight or fret when God's hand is at work. Trust Him, He knows what's best for you. And if we say that we believe in Him, we must believe Him. So praise God when tribulation knocks at the door. Be armored up and ready, the task and time is at hand. God is ready to use you and elevate you. Glory be to the Father, who could have chosen anyone, who could have created anything to worship and reverence Him.

But He chose me.

## *To My Brothers…*

Dear Brothers,

Hold on. God is working. He is cultivating a queen. One specifically for you. One who will serve you as she values serving the Lord. One who understands that God is pleased by her obedience in His instructions for her to be your help-meet. Take your spirit and drive to conquer to search the depths of God's heart to find the treasures that He has hidden deep, specifically for you. He gave you the mind of a king and the determination of a hunter to equip you for the journey that life delivers. Be patient, be obedient, and unveil the royalty that He set aside for you. It is a treasure that is not easily discovered, because if it were it would be for everyone instead of divinely set apart for you. Don't be distracted by idleness. Look around you. If the pleasures of the world are her pearls, run. Seek, pray, ask, and wait. The only way to recognize the prize that God has created for you to build a legacy and continue a lineage with, is to become that legacy and lineage within yourself. This will not come easy. Because if it were so, everyone would have discovered it. Become that longing and love that you desire, dress yourself in salvation. Protect your soul with honesty. Guard your lineage with obedience. Hide your heart with wisdom. Create your masterpiece with love. And build your kingdom with perseverance. Wait.

Hold on my brothers. Hold on.

*Inspiration*

## <u>To My Sisters...</u>

Dear Women,

Hold on. Be patient. Keep striving and elevating. There is a man, who is waiting for a woman who is meek, gentle, patient and mature. There is a king who is searching for a queen. Not one whose concerns are worldly. Not one whose riches are in her car, clothes and career. But a godly woman. A rare breed. One who examines his strengths and his weaknesses. Who loves him inside then out. Who prays and fasts and patiently waits on instruction from God. One whom he can trust. One whom he knows will make decisions for he and his family based off of her direction from God. One who isn't driven by her "feelings" but by her spirit. Don't be discouraged by those that walk away. They see that royalty requires loyalty and their weakness is married to intimidation. Laziness. Complacency. And selfishness. This is a quest for the strong and the conscious. Consider their neglect as a benefit. Praise God at the defeat of the enemies attempts to dress as a sheep in wolves clothing. There is a man. One who is searching for a woman who possesses long-suffering, kindness, loyalty, pride and unconditional love. One who takes her time, learning him through different seasons and areas of his life. One who wholeheartedly embraces the good as well as the bad. One who's strength is seen and not heard. One who is slow to speak and quick to listen. One who runs from malice and takes hold to truth. One whom he can trust. One whom he knows will hold steadfast to the guidance of God, and not man. One who will cling to the instruction of God no matter how hard things get. One who when the world around her falls, will stand. All while learning, growing and cultivating her craft. Not allowing idleness to eat away at her value. Bathing in purity and clothing with dignity. Covering her head with righteousness and her feet with love.

Hold on my sister. Hold on.

*Inspiration*

## **<u>The Choice</u>**

And just like that, it hit me!

Life isn't hard because God "made" it this way.

Life is hard because we have chosen for it to be this way.

Each individual decision that we as humans have ever made, have all added up to the place that we are at this very moment.

God's intentions were never for us to experience any hurt and harm.

We decided that we did not want to live God's way.

We wanted to try living our own way.

We believed that we may have known just a little more than our creator.

He loves us so much that He gave us exactly what we wanted.

Since the fall of man, we decided to live our own way instead of Gods.

Because we can only comprehend so much, we made mistake after mistake.

Some which could have ended our species as a whole.

But time after time God stepped in and saved us from our own ignorance.

The barrier of protection was lifted.

He gave us the freedom of choice.

## Follow My Pen

We chose to leave His covering.

Since then we have been on a journey of discovery.

One that continues to lead us back to the place that we started out at.

Back to a place of protection and covering.

Now we long for a world of peace and prosperity.

But when we had it we wanted to know what it would be like to find something else.

Now we spend our lives, longing for Him to have His way.

Because we do not know the way.

But God loves us so much.

So much that He has always given us what we wanted.

God is so merciful that He derived a plan.

He gave us another chance.

A chance to learn, grow and become who we were destined and created to be.

Now we go through hell searching for heaven.

Because when we had heaven we wanted to know hell.

*Inspiration*

## ***A Fresh Start...***

*"Those who are well have no need of a physician, but those who are sick..."*

***Luke 5:31***

So many times I (we) get down on ourselves about making mistakes, or not being perfect. God assures us that He sent His son Jesus Christ to earth specifically for you and I. God delights in our weaknesses because they magnify His strengths. He never asked us to be perfect, He's asking us to give all of our shortcomings, downfalls, hardships and problems to Him. He wants to take them and make them into our testimony, for someone else. Imagine the artwork that is made out of madness... Life would be mundane if we had no trials, and ups and downs. How could we grow if we weren't stretched beyond what we know? Greatness is birthed from great things and that does not happen by simply existing. So praise God for your tribulations and embrace the journey. Be honored that you get to follow in the footsteps of the Messiah, and as He has shown us, when the road gets tough think about the destination that awaits ahead.

Be blessed!

*"I have not come to call the righteous, but sinners, to repentance..."*

***Luke 5:32***

Follow My Pen

## **The Answers**

Why as humans do we feel we have all the answers?...

Who told us that the mark stopped with us?...

We don't even know why we are here...

We do not get to choose our sex and to whom we are given to...

We can not explain the changes in our world...

We can't describe the parts of the ocean we have not seen...

We cannot fathom the galaxies of the sky that cannot be imagined...

How many times have we thought that a road would lead us in one direction only to end up in another?...

How many failures have we endured despite our hard work and faith?...

How many have we lost no matter how much we wanted to save?...

How many have strayed no matter how much we gave?...

All we can do is try...

All we can hope...

All we can do is wait...

No more will I listen to the voices of the world...

*Inspiration*

Everything I need is within in me…

Every move and decision must come from a place from within…

An indescribable depth…

A voice so deep within my soul that it overcomes me…

        I am searching…

        I am praying…

        I am asking…

        I am waiting…

        For the answers.

## Life + Death

It's crazy how we really do not see the full circle, meaning and purpose of someone's journey until they have finished it, and in some cases some purposes aren't fulfilled until after death, i.e. Jesus Christ, who in death saved the lives of those before and after Him. The bible tells us that we will not know or understand the full meaning of life until we meet our creator face-to-face. This life is such a deep and mysterious existence. It has so many options and choices, so many places to go, things to do and people to meet. It's strange when you think about it… It sort of reminds me of a video game with unlimited resources and levels. Death did not settle into my heart the way it now has until I lost someone near and dear to me. I have lost many loved-ones but some hit closer to home than others and some deaths bring out feelings and emotions that you may have never known existed. Life can have this affect as well. For example, the love that I experienced when my little sister was born, has been the most amazing experience of life that I have encountered to this day in my life. I have experienced and witnessed the births of four nephews and one niece, whom I love more than life, but none have affected me the way my little sisters birth did. In a way, I felt as though she was my own child, so for those that have children, I have been told, that the birth of your own child is thee absolute greatest love you will ever feel, and I pray that I get to experience that kind of love one day. The bible tells us that in death we may live.

*"A good name is better than fine perfume, and the day of death better than the day of birth."*

***Ecclesiastes 7:1***

This was hard to grasp because I had so many emotions piled on top of this understanding that no matter how much I wanted to and needed to believe in this, I could not find my way. I was angry, hurt, and felt betrayed by God because I knew that He knew how much I loved and how sad I would be, but yet He still allowed death to come and take my loved-one away. Sometimes I still think about it and find myself questioning God, but more of the peace comes in, which comes from Him, and comforts me with the truth that He shared with us to help us during these inevitable times. A realization that I have come to throughout this entire of experience of losing someone so close to me is that now death has a different appearance in my life. Although it still saddens me, and sometimes I feel afraid of the thoughts and that they will no longer be with us, deaths pierce does not hurt the way that it did before. In a sense, I envy those that have completed this journey. They no longer have to fight and experience the trials of life. Their souls are resting peacefully. As life continues, I now see that it is short, and sweet. The good times and the bad, the ups and the downs all come together to display a beautiful masterpiece of triumph and overcome. For those that are gone, job well done, for those still striving to make it to the promised land, keep fighting, keep going, hold on, don't give up, we can make it. Let the lives of those who have come and gone be an example, a motivation and a light.

*"But I would not have you to be ignorant, brethren, concerning them which are asleep, that ye sorrow not, even as others which have no hope.*

*For if we believe that Jesus died and rose again, even so them also which sleep in Jesus will God bring with him.*

*For this we say unto you by the word of the Lord, that we which are alive [and] remain unto the coming of the Lord shall not prevent them which are asleep.*

*For the Lord himself shall descend from heaven with a shout, with the voice of the archangel, and with the trump of God: and the dead in Christ shall rise first:*

*Then we which are alive [and] remain shall be caught up together with them in the clouds, to meet the Lord in the air: and so shall we ever be with the Lord.*

*Wherefore comfort one another with these words."*

***1 Thessalonians Chapter 4:13-18***

*Inspiration*

## **<u>Discovery</u>**

Today's enlightenment truly brought joy to my heart... Because my Father, God, continues to show me who and whose I am. There are many things that I don't know or understand about myself, but with prayer, silence and patience, God is constantly revealing one thing after another, peeling back one layer after another. With that being said, today's verse was shared to me by a fellow follower who reminded me that we are to be helpers one of another, so I am sharing it with you. It brought laughter to me because the smallest things about me, that I don't even understand, become so clear and meaningful through the word of God, our Father. So enjoy this passage written by King Solomon, I found it to be quite amusing, as God can often be!

*"Don't visit your neighbors too often, or you will wear out your welcome. Telling lies about others is as harmful as hitting them with an ax, wounding them with a sword, or shooting them with a sharp arrow. Putting confidence in an unreliable person is like chewing with a toothache or walking on a broken foot. Singing cheerful songs to a person whose heart is heavy is as bad as stealing someone's jacket in cold weather or rubbing salt in a wound. If your enemies are hungry, give them food to eat. If they are thirsty, give them water to drink. You will heap burning coals on their heads, and the LORD will reward you. As surely as a wind from the north brings rain, so a gossiping tongue causes anger! It is better to live alone in the corner of an attic than with a contentious wife in a lovely home. Good news from far away is like cold water to the thirsty. If the godly compromise with the wicked, it is like polluting a fountain or muddying a spring. Just as it is not good to eat too much honey, it is not good for people to think about all the honors they deserve."*

Follow My Pen

***Proverbs 25:17-27***

*Inspiration*

## **Spirit. Soul. Body.**

We as people encounter so much just throughout the course of one day, let alone a lifetime if you are blessed to experience what one truly is. Taking care of your spirit, soul and body are key components in living a healthy, balanced and effective life. One cannot excel without the other. The body needs the soul, the soul needs the spirit and the spirit needs the body. Taking care of oneself means more than just taking a shower, being nice and going to church. One must actually get to know each component and its personality in order to know just how to provide each one's specific needs. Just as important as it is to not subject your body to many different people and things, our soul and spirit are the same way. The spirit and soul cannot simply be submerged into water to wash away its impurities, like the body can. The spirit and soul are much more sensitive requiring much more attention and care. The soul, which is also known as the personality, changes, so if you don't spend quality time getting to know yours constantly how will you know what it needs?... And more importantly, how will you know it at all?... People spend a lot of time talking about the past, what happened, what didn't in life, filling their spiritual space with other people and things, using them as a crutch, or what I like to call an excuse, to not change and grow. What happened to you when you were born, six years old, growing up and even yesterday are all gone, evaporated, it has disappeared, vanished. Instead of leaning on old, molded ways (crutches) to make excuses for not making changes that you're afraid or too lazy to make, realize that these things all happened, occurred and took place to place you exactly where God intended for you to be at this very moment in your life. Your past and even your present are choices in which you will either allow to change you or hinder you. Grow up!! You will either seize the day around you or miss out on it because you are still living in yesterday.

Some people will spend their entire lives never knowing who they are and what they could be. Don't be that person! This life is a gift, this body is what you do with it, this soul is what you make it, and this spirit is what you allow it.

***Be blessed!***

*Inspiration*

## **The Journey to Discovery**

God visited a little boy one day and asked him, "Son, what would you like to be when you grow up?" The little boy replied, "Well, I don't know…" So God asked the little boy, "When you wake up in the morning what's the first thing on your mind?" The little boy replied, "Well I like climbing trees… I want to be a tree when I grow up!" Then God said, "Throughout the day what do you think about the most?" The little boy replied, "Well, I like bugs and animals…. When I grow up I want to be a horse!" God replied, "What do you dream about when you go to sleep at night?" The little boy sat for a second and looked up at the sky… "I think about the stars and the moon!" And with a burst of excitement the little boy answered, "When I grow up I want to be the moon!" Then God smiled and looked at His son and said, "Well my son, although I created the trees, and told them to grow big and strong so that they would provide you with oxygen to breathe, shade from the rays of the sun, and shelter for the animals, if you become one who will plant more so that when you grow up little boys like yourself can climb them too? When I created horses I told them to run like the wind, to be of service and be under the command of man, so if you become one, who will take care of you, and how will you take care of them so when you grow up little boys like yourself can ride them as well? When I made the moon and the stars I marveled upon their beauty and brightness and was pleased, if you become the moon you will be the brother to the sun, providing light to the night, but who will give spiritual direction to the people. Who will help the blind, heal the sick and unbelieving, and who will lead the way for the lost? Who will share these conversations between you and I with the generations to come? Who will pass along the wisdom and knowledge that you have and will gain?" The little boy sat silent for a moment in deep thought… Then he asked God, "Well what should I be?" And God lovingly answered, "All of the things around you that you love so much are because I placed them in you while I was creating you. Long before your mother ever knew she would give birth to you I spent time on every detail of your existence. I spent time getting to know everything you would ever know and want to be so that I could guide you and help you go in the direction that I created you to go in." The little boy began to understand more clearly as God continued to speak to him. "This is why it is important to listen to your spirit because that is my voice speaking to and leading you. There is a reason why an artist notices certain things that a scientist may not. It is because of what I have placed in that artist and in the scientist to affect and fulfill. This ensure that there is a balance and that all aspects of this earth and your spiritual needs are met. Do you understand now?" God asked… The little boy jumped to his feet and gave God a big hug. God smiled at the little boy and the little boy said, "Thank you God!!!" God asked, "Why are you thanking me?" And the little boy replied, "Because you love me so much that although you created the trees to help me live and the horses to help me run and the moon to help me see, You created me! And in Your image." God grew more and more proud of his son in that moment. "Now I know what I want to be when I grow up!" God asked, "And what is that my son?" And the little boy replied, "A man of You! The best ME that I can possibly be! Firmer than a tree, stronger than a horse, shinning brighter than the moon!" God was pleased, and He gave the little boy exactly what He asked for.

*The beauty is not in BEing everything around you, the beauty is in CHANGing everything around you. Find YOURSELF, know YOURSELF, and BE YourSelf! Do not CONform, TRANSform!*

*Inspiration*

**God bless!!!**

## **<u>My Kind of Love</u>**

When the sun does not shine,

When the tide is too high,

When the lights have gone down,

When the well has run dry,

When the moon hides behind the clouds,

When the dusk won't turn to dawn,

When the leaves have all fallen,

When the flowers and fruit are gone,

When the cold rules the land,

When the warmth is nowhere in sight,

When there's nothing left to say,

When the noon turns into night,

When the cares have faded away,

When there is no one to call,

When those you thought were there for you, can't seem to be found at all,

*Inspiration*

When the soul begins to listen,

When the pride turns into meek,

When familiarity comes up missing,

When the heart begins to speak,

When your head has hung low,

The only direction to look is above,

That's when all around, you will feel my kind of love.

***Be blessed!***

## **The High Road**

*"Good sense makes one slow to anger,
and it is his glory to overlook an offense."*

**Proverbs 19:11**

This scripture gave me joy this morning and was motivation to address an issue that I find to be more and more dominant in my social circles, as well as in society. I feel as though I have been having this conversation more often lately than I ever have… So it is no coincidence that God would show up with His infinite wisdom.

In a time where self-expression overrules standard, knowledge is a necessity. Expression can be an art that is abused, if not used correctly, or maturely, as any other gift or talent. Yes, we all have a voice, but for this very reason we all must know when and how to use it. With social media presence in such a high demand, so many people feel the need to inform the world on every move they make and every step they take, yet they wonder why their peace is constantly being interrupted. I ask myself all the time, "Who do these people think they are?…" But that goes for the offended as well as the offender. When we give our opinion we open ourselves up to opinion. That is just the way it goes. No, this does not mean be a loner and keep to yourself, it just means be wise about your decisions because what we say has a lifetime effect on not only others but ourselves. Think about it, in order to spew poison from one's lips, the poison has to come *from* one's lips!… Meaning, if you say hateful and evil things to someone, that same hate and evil is inside of you, which makes you no better than the other person… In fact, it makes you worse.

With the amount of unnecessary drama our society is constantly surrounded by, which are distractions and tricks of the enemy, and during a time where it is hard and scarce to find an outer peace, you would think more people would have no choice but to look inside of themselves to search for a solution to the problem. But instead we take that same hatred, hurt and pain that we feel and we slander and crucify others with that same evil. Jesus told His companion,

*"Put away your sword, those who use the sword will die by the sword."*

### Matthew 26:52

I believe this was purposed literally and figuratively. Our sword can be our tongue. In fact, the bible says:

*"The words of the reckless pierce like swords, but the tongue of the wise brings healing." Proverbs 12:18 "They sharpen their tongues like swords and aim cruel words like deadly arrows."*

### Psalm 64:3

If you are the person who always feels the need to" keep it real," and "express" how you feel, do not be surprised when your life is constantly filled with drama, confusion and misfortune.

It does not make you any less of a person to be slow to speak and quick to hear and slow to anger.

*"My dear brothers and sisters, take note of this: Everyone should be quick to listen, slow to speak and slow to become angry."*

***James 1:19***

As a matter of fact, it shows wisdom and maturity when one is able to control their anger and emotions and stand firm in who they are and not waiver when tribulations or transgressions are thrown his/her way.

*"Whoever is slow to anger is better than the mighty, and he who rules his spirit than he who takes a city."*

***Proverbs 16:32***

The enemy has always specialized in deceit, planting seeds of the exact opposite of what God instructs us to do. God's plans are for prosper and the enemies are for persecution. Satan is the originator of the term "hater" and those feelings of pride and arrogance that convince us that our way is the right and only way, and our opinion *has* to be heard, are all fruits of evil, not of God, and result in self-destruction.

*"For I know the plans I have for you," declares the LORD, "plans to prosper you and not to harm you, plans to give you hope and a future."*

***Jeremiah 29:11***

Keeping it "real" doesn't win you any cool points with God. Look to our ultimate exemplification of honor, humility and integrity, Jesus Christ. He was a direct descendant of God, a king and savior of all mankind, and he took the lowest role possible here on earth. He was homeless, but blameless persecuted put pure, and he kept His mouth shut, His eyes forward, His heart pure.

*Inspiration*

The best analogy that I have been able to give is this: If a direct decision does not better the world, you as an individual, add hours to your life, money to your account, or make the sun shine any brighter is it really worth the couple seconds of energy or anger that you give, and cannot get back?… If that answer is "no" keep it moving. It's not your battle anyway, it's the Lords. And that battle has already been won. ; )

*"For we wrestle not against flesh and blood, but against principalities, against powers, against the rulers of the darkness of this world, against spiritual wickedness in high places."*

**Ephesians 6:12**

*"This battle is not yours. It's the Lords!"*

**Be Blessed.**

## **No Greater Love**

Father, I thank you!

You have been so good to me.

I don't know why you love me.

But I know you do!

I was afraid that you wouldn't know I love you,

Because my ways have not always been true,

But today you told me that's its ok,

Because the one consistency in my life is you,

Now I realize that you have always been there,

And you promised you would never leave,

No matter how I fall, or how many times I fail,

You always bring me back to you,

One thing that I can promise no matter what where I go or what I do,

Is that I will always come back to you.

Your love never fails and never gives up,

So I am learning to love and be more like you.

*Inspiration*

I will fight and strive and stays at your feet,

Until face-to-face, you and I will meet.

Thank you Father, there truly is none like you.

Your love is perfects me. It transforms me thru and thru.

Without even knowing, your will has always won,

And my heart, my life and my all belongs to you!

Thank you Jesus!!!

## "Fathers Be Good to Your Daughters"

As I hand-washed my car this afternoon I began to reflect on my dad, and all of the things I have learned from him. I started at the back of my car and began hearing his voice in my heart, reminding me to wash the car in sections... As I proceeded to the back door I started to wash the tires and I remembered, the tires take some time and detail so to wash those last so that the soap didn't start to dry on the car... So I quickly moved back up to the door and began washing just the back of the body and so on and so forth. I started reminiscing on many things my father has taught me and I wanted to share with men out there that the magnitude a father's love has on a daughter is indescribable. My dad's strength and perseverance has taught me to fight, be strong and never give up, no matter what life throws my way. His honesty and fearlessness has taught me to be just and fair, and stand in the face of adversity, knowing who and who's I am. His spirit has taught me to be silent, listen, be patient and make sound judgement. He taught me to pay attention to detail and be independent; if no one else will do it for you, you always have yourself. His commitment taught me loyalty and longevity. His "I love yous" make me feel beautiful and his "You're beautifuls" let me know that I am truly loved. I know that he means it. He has seen me grow, learn, make mistakes, make stupid decisions, be foolish, immature, experiment, fall, get up, become stronger, and be passionate. So when he tells me that I am a princess, I believe him, because to know all there is about me; my fears and tears and still pray for the best; even when I disappoint him he hopes for the best; is patient with my journey; helps me along the way; is there for me; gives me honesty and truth, his love is the realest love one could ever receive from a man... and it started at birth, at home, before any other voice or influence could rebuttal or reject it, manipulate it or neglect it... It was there and it's never going anywhere. So for all of his sacrifices, long nights, tears, prayers and strength, **thank you**! Your love means more to me than any other man on this earth could ever even begin to imagine.

***Thank you!!***

## **Love Lifted Me**

Driving home last night it began to sprinkle a light rain. I looked around and it was as if I was the only one experiencing it. Suddenly my inner peace started to speak and the question arose, "What if these were Jesus' tears?" I immediately became sorrowful and started reflecting on His purity and how much He's given and sacrificed. I was overcome with the thought of Him sitting on the thrown in heaven, still working and laboring for His people. Still interceding and intervening for our well-being. Time after time I've hurt him and still continue to. But He continues to love me, to care for me, to nurture me, and lead me. I was faced with this question, "Is love enough?" I believe it is. I believe when selfish ways are set aside and when truth outshines lies, love is the only things that will survive. I truly believe that love *will* prevail, because it has no choice but to. It will be the strongest and withstanding entity, it will grow stronger and taller with each blow, with each lie, with every being that has tried to tear it down. Love will survive all that is currently competing for our minds. Even in hatred there will be love, even in death there will be love. When all has faded and everything has passed on. Love will live, on, long and strong.

*Inspiration*

## **Wake Up**

We live in a time where people are afraid to live, afraid to love and afraid to give.

Where money rules our minds, are hearts are spoiled and sour, our chest is exposed and open, handed to the enemy on a platter to devour.

A time where hurt, pain and tears are matched with lies, evil and fears. Where our minds are being manipulated, revealed but not being healed.

Where wrong is right and right is wrong, where the world says live fast and not long; and to love is weak and to give is dumb; where it's me, myself and I, and sympathy is numb.

Where creation is trying to be recreated meanwhile souls are being cremated. Lips lie and eyes are blind. Where honesty, integrity and obedience are hard to find.

A time of bust, lust and disgust. Shame, fame and no trust. No loyalty, more hurt and manipulation. Pointing the blame instead of providing the education.

Killing the soul instead of healing the soul. Total damnation is the enemy's goal. No love just lust, no loyalty, no trust, no remorse, just hate, we must suffer through this turmoil until that special date. And for the ones who thought time was irrelevant it will be too late. Judgment will be proclaimed and evildoers must face their fate. And for those who fought the good fight the ending will be great.

**Stay encouraged!**

Follow My Pen

## **Feel**

Feel my heart

Feel my soul

Feel my art

*Fill my whole*

Feel my highs

Feel my lows

Feel my ups

Feel my downs

Feel my smiles

Feel my frowns

Feel my truths

Feel my lies

Feel my laughter

Feel my cries

Feel my failure

Feel my wins

*Inspiration*

Feel my purity

Feel my sins

Feel my max

Feel my min

Feel my rough

Feel my smooth

Feel my tough

Feel my groove

Feel my poverty

Feel my wealth

Feel my sickness

Feel my health

Feel my fears

Feel my doubt's

Feel my whispers

Feel my shouts

Follow My Pen

Feel my ins

Feel my outs

Feel my depths

Feel my peaks

Feel my takes

Feel my keeps

Feel my yes

Feel my no

Feel my stop

Feel my go

Feel my stagnant

Feel my grow

Feel my energy

Feel my life

Feel my love

Feel my breath

*Inspiration*

Feel my spirit

Feel my death.

.

# Follow My Pen

*Inspiration*

## Follow My Pen

"Certain individuals have been gifted with a presence when they enter into the room. Some other people are gifted with the ability to leave you with a certain appreciation and love... when they leave you. It is as if some of their "superpower" has rubbed off on you--and you are grateful that it has. Tiffani Addison, poet, writer, and author, happens to be a person that does both: she has a presence when she walks in the room and she leaves you with love and the thought, I can do anything but fail! This same spirit flows through her art, where she grants license for the reader to be, speak, write, create, and do, any and all good things. The self-defined, *Passionista*, lover of all good things, Tiffani Addison, is more than a mere writer; she is a creative artist who has gained experience within the avenues of radio, television, print and online magazine and newspapers, fashion and sports, just to name a few. But simple pen and paper, always seem to find their home with the www.FollowMyPen creator. Her topic of choice you quickly find evident in a one-on-one encounter with her: Light. Tiffani aims to spread light and empower people to live the life that God created them for."

-Nicole Brown, creator of *Overtaken*

I believe that my art is a breath of fresh air in today's society. I am not pushing trends or opinions on anyone, or trying to promote myself of being seen. I remain in my lane of just inspiring, motivating and encouraging others through knowledge, inspiration and poetry. The Holy Spirit will drop a topic in my heart and usually over the course of, sometimes one day up to a couple of month, I will see and hear pieces that trigger that thought. The thoughts continue to build on one another, eventually, leaving me with an overflow of words and emotions that I have to "get out" on paper. Growing up I witnessed women without a voice, and I personally experienced being misunderstood for a very long time. Once I got a taste of freedom, I spread my wings and I flew and that has inspired me to show and teach women that they can never let anything take their voice away, it is their unique gift from God. So whatever your voice is, whether it is art, cooking; cosmetology; writing, or engineering, spread your wings and fly. I believe that seeing art as life is the only way to look at it. Art is all around us and in everything we do. The way we breathe, how our bodies function, how we see the exact same things throughout the day but interpret them differently, art is all around us, we are art! Having people tell me that my words had them in tears or that they felt a certain emotion from reading my writing has impacted me the most. The tangible evidence that the same spirit I felt when creating, is what is passed through my words to readers is powerful and helps me remain accountable in being a vessel. What I like most about my work is that I can say that it is truly organic. I write from the soul. If what I have to say is not received well I still have no regrets because I am patient and attentive to what I discern and what is given to me. It is the truth, the whole truth and nothing but, and because of that I feel relieved once I have expressed myself. It feels like that task has been completed and I wait for the next one. My dream project is to complete a series of books that inspire, women of all ages; from little girls to elderly women. I want to spark a fire in them that cannot be put out. I want to give them the tools that they need to eliminate the distractions of this world and live in the fullness and greatness that God intended for us to.

With love, Tiffani R. Addison

*"You are the salt of the earth; but if the salt has become tasteless, how can it be made salty again? It is no longer good for anything, except to be thrown out and trampled underfoot by men. "You are the light of the world. A city set on a hill cannot be hidden; nor does anyone light a lamp and put it under a basket, but on the lampstand, and it gives light to all who are in the house...."*
*Matthew 5:13-14*

# FOLLOW MY PEN

*Inspiration* is an expression of daily prayers and devotions to and from God, in poetry, knowledge and inspirational thoughts through my pen. My prayer is that you have been inspired and that you go and inspire someone in return.

*Inspiration. Knowledge. Poetry*

Made in the USA
Lexington, KY
01 November 2016